Min Hyun Sik

Min Hyun Sik

Architecture 1987–2012

Translated by Pai Hyungmin

Youlhwadang

When I read, I jot down words and draw things between the lines and the blank spaces of the page. When I am particularly immersed in a certain book, I use separate memo sheets like Post-It. In order to remember the circumstances of that moment, I may write on receipts, envelopes, and tickets. As a way of reorganizing "the order of the book" into "the structure of my thinking," the simultaneous act of reading and moving my hand is actually a means to engrave the book not only onto my mind but also onto my body. These jottings become traces that remain in my mind and body, and the memory of the book reemerges when I am searching through the book again. The accumulation of these traces is the accumulation of my thinking and the beginning of my architecture.

Min Hyun Sik

· This is the English translation of the original Korean edition published in 2012. It is the author's first portfolio of selected architectural work from 1987 to 2012.

· The texts in the book provide the foundation of the author's architectural thinking and do not necessarily have a direct relation to the adjacent photograph of the author's work.

· The specific sources of quotations are listed in the "Quotation Sources" at the end of the book. Texts without source notations are those of the author's.

Contents

Paul Bourget said that "One must live the way one thinks, or end up thinking the way one has lived." These words were the catalyst in forming my idea of *the space of self-discipline*.

The great architects of history, particularly the masters of twentieth century modernism, were like dictators. They deemed all architecture that did not determine everyday-life to be useless. Mies van der Rohe, for example, declared that "the struggle for new housing is only an element of the larger struggle for new forms of living." The modern masters began with pure intentions, but as things quickly got out of hand, they held on to a sanctity by manipulating a despondent humanity.

We see this situation rehearsed in Song Ki Won's cautionary words addressed to Ha Jong Oh.

He has denied his own limitations in regard to the people. In the narrative section of his second collection of poems, he sings directly of their lives through the perspective of the peasant, the street cleaner, and the urban poor living in land fills. Here and there, we discover works in which artistry and poetic tension have been totally undone. More troublesome is the fact that his view of the people has too easily fallen prey to moralism and idealism. Is not moralism, idealism, and over-theorization the first symptoms of poets and intellectuals estranged from reality? (···) Too much affection is bound to hide the truth. (···) True poets will eventually return and plant their roots. There, poets write with hands dirtied by soil, rust, and manure. Ha Jong Oh should not return alone. The poets of this land must all return to that place. The happy times are over.

If we understand that the task of today's architect is not the creation of *a building-thing* that designs life but the coordination of everyday events and spatial *relations*, we then need a wisdom that embraces opposites. Architecture, like the city, should not be materialized as a thing but perceived as a process.

The *madang* is like the electronic system
of a microchip board hidden behind
its casing. It has neither beginning
nor end and its essence lies in its ever-
changing and flowing dynamics.

Mies van der Rohe has said that "If you view nature through the glass walls of the Farnsworth House, it gains a more profound significance than if viewed from out side. That way more is said about nature—it becomes a part of a larger whole." We may repeat these words as we look out from the Mandae-ru Pavilion in Byeongsan Seowon Academy because we can agree with Fritz Neumeyer that what is most effective in architecture is not form but space (*der Raum*) and emptiness (*das Leere*).

The arguments that architecture has always
been subservient to the ruling authorities
in human society (Pier Vittorio Aureli) or
that the domination of space is the source
of social power and that the history of
mankind is the history of spatial struggle
(Henri Lefebvre) are extremely persuasive.
However, today's architectural ethics must
understand Rem Koolhaas' statement
that "architecture is a dangerous mixture
of power and impotence" and minimize
the influence of these statements.

Movement in the *madang* does not
require hierarchy or system. Movement
ever slightly deviates from its anticipated
flow, presenting at each of these moments
an unanticipated, specific landscape. As
we move along, the boundary between
inner and outer space dissolves, creating
a captivating field of contradiction and
tension. It is not a particularly special
landscape. On the contrary, the landscape
of the everyday is seen in a new way. A
very low frame shows the lightness of
the affluent city. A line of trees stand out
along the background of the neighboring
wall. Their barks light up the picturesque
landscape. Look up from a narrow alley.
Their walls suddenly expose their particular
materiality and we awake freshened by a
piece of the urban sky. The combination
of scenes are precisely edited along our

movement. They are akin to a series of still photographs compiled as a video. They have the strength to awaken our daily lives.

Hence the relationship between the *madang* and life is dynamic, always giving rise to conflict. This is the essential character of everyday life. Life lies not within the space. It is dissolved in the space, as if engraved on it, and thus moves independently with the space. When the life of a temporary occupancy ends, we anticipate a crisis that the space will altogether collapse. However, as we witness the aura created by every encounter, we know that the sustainable quality of the space persists within.

This is possible not because of the purposeful design of the *madang* but because of the design of conditions and relationships. Here, the distinction between space and life is irrelevant. Rather than temporarily accommodating life, space itself, with the help of life, creates an atmosphere unique for the moment. We are not just stepping on the ground of a new space; we are rather entering the space, at every moment creating conflict until space and life are united and stabilized.

The traditional thought of Korea consistently demonstrates a beautiful and profound ecological wisdom. It is a poetic and aesthetic mode of thought. It goes beyond narrow anthropocentricism and pronounces that man and nature, man and the universe are fundamentally the same being. It sings the rhythms of life by following the principle that *the universe ceaselessly creates man and things.*

—Park Hee Byeong

I call this idea of modernity a myth because the notion of a radical break has a certain persuasive and pervasive power in the face of abundant evidence that it does not, and can not, possibly occur. (···) No social order can achieve changes that are not already latent within its existing condition.

This is David Harvey's clear logic that instantly reverses modernism's directive of *creative destruction.*

Following an abstracted topography, platforms are layed out in sequence to form *the infrastructure of life.* These platforms sustain potential. Their flexibility has been maximized in order to move beyond simple function. They hence become a system that responds quickly and appropriately to the rapidly changing needs of the society and its times. This is an architectural practice exercised by the innate logic of the land.

Streets and pathways are mankind's
greatest and most consistent attempt to
transform the passage of time, as part of its
irrevocable destiny, into an architectural
structure. Transforming the memory
of the past into the present, the street
is filled with flaneurs casually taking
pleasure in the dialectical transformation
of the fragments of various things and
events into another image. The pathway
is a place of *that* which harmonizes
seemingly contradictory values.

As Chun Jin Sung argues: "Memory is (…)
the mental (psychological) phenomena
of transforming an individual's past
into the present." That is, it is the
subject's mental act and process of
relating his past to the present. "History
is not simply the aggregation of the
past but an objective process where the
subjective consciousness *of* the past is
played out. To state it succinctly, it is a
history of *historical consciousness.*"

The value to be retrieved is more
health than beauty. The ethics of
architectural design consists in finding
the solution for an ecological, economic,
geographical, and philosophical state of
health. And when this value gains the
sympathy of those who live within this
architecture, it becomes even healthier.

I have seen at other times and in other places many scriptoria, but none where there shone so luminously, in the outpouring, of physical light which made the room glow, the spiritual principle that light incarnates, radiance, source of all beauty and learning, inseparable attribute of that proportion the room embodied. For three things concur in creating beauty: first of all integrity or perfection, and for this reason we consider ugly all incomplete things; then proper proportion or consonance; and finally clarity and light, and in fact we call beautiful those things of definite color.

—Umberto Eco, *The Name of the Rose*

Architecture is simultaneously a product of
social relations and a dynamic object that
is in continuous counter-action with social
processes. In this sense, the architectural work
makes us walk the path that they had walked;
it makes us see the landscape of moutains and
streams that they had seen. It is thus that we
turn a close ear to the words of Luis Barragán.

Don't ask me about this building
or that one, don't look at what I do.
See what I saw.

In the case of the Charles de Gaulle airport, as a city that exists for the purpose of circulation, its sole meaning lies in the overlapping and interlocking of *networks*. Therefore, it is city that does not require the distinction between building and road. As you point out, urban infrastructure is the key in La Défense, where the building exists merely as a peripheral cell.

From this perspective, our work consists of creating the meta-structure that prefigures the structure of the buildings and roads.

In this method of thinking, because there is no telling how far the building's *program*—considered as the last line of defense—will change or may even disappear, the method of *mapping* must now change. When this happens, architecture is not the act of covering the program with a shell but the creation of a different kind of story.

—Chang Yong Soon and Min Hyun Sik

The nature that we encounter everyday in the city and in architecture is one whose primordial form has already been greatly transformed. My hope is that with time, nature and artifice, rather than being at odds with each other, will melt into each other and evolve together. In this artificial nature, with the artificial environment gradually responding in specific fashion to this evolution, architectural work simultaneously abstracts this situation and thereby generalizes the situation and secures its modernity. Through such abstractions it seeks to approximate nature's original structure. We may call such an intentional artificial figure an *architectural landscape.*

Architecture is a (small) city that sustains within itself an urban program and spatial organization. There is a decisive choice to be made. Should it be an environmentally-determined city, a social condenser with socially-engineered programs? Or should it be a Synoikismos, Aristotles's ideal city—a city of decentralized democracy where diverse values co-exist within a community? Or should it be what Francois Ascher has called the *metapolis*: an urban community of multi-layered and multi-dimensional democracy?

If we were to choose the latter, the form of the city would not be defined visually or just by a few buildings. Here, monumental architecture or symbolic objects can no longer function as agents of the urban environment. An age that requires symbolic monuments is an age of propaganda and slogans; it is a barbaric society.

I want to build a house in which past and future become a continuous present. It is identical to Yevgeny Vinokurov's wish to write such a book.

> Sometimes, I'd like to write a book
> A book all about time
> About how it doesn't exist,
> How the past and future
> Are one continuous present.
> I think that all people—those living,
>   those who have lived
> And those who are still to live—are alive
>   now.
> I should like to take that subject to pieces,
> Like a soldier dismantling his rifle.

Detail lies at the center of making spaces that can be appropriated through the five senses. Though the primary function of detail is the smooth connection of material and material, space and space, in actuality, they function within the transformations of situation and time. Light, color, sound, smell, texture, and taste. Detail is a mechanism that measures these senses and makes us aware of them. It is a frame that motivates the viewer to gladly confront the changes in the object. It is my wish that through the force of the detail the relation between people who float from space to space assimilates the fine subtlety of Agnes Martin's hyper-abstractions.

The detail that places Gwangpung-gak Pavilion in Soswewon Garden so delicately within nature is a detail that fulfills its role. Here, it is a mechanism that invites light and wind, sound and smell. That is why the pavilion is called *a house of dancing light and wind* in the *garden of clean air*.

We keep something empty so as not to presume a ready-made emotion. We do this with the hope that when a certain space, place, or formal object is set within a specific condition, a unique condition and feeling will be created at every moment.

In this sense, Louis Kahn is for me an excellent textbook.

> We knew that the museum (building) would always be full of surprises. The blues would be one thing one day; the blues would be another thing another day, depending on the character of the light. Nothing static, nothing static as an electric bulb, which can only give you one iota of the character of light. So the museum (building) has as many moods as there are moments in time, and never as long as the museum remains as a building will there be a single day like the other. (⋯)
>
> A great American poet once asked the architect, "What slice of the sun does your building have? What light enters your room?"—As if to say the sun never knew how great it is until it struck the side of a building.

What we know about things is not
through their own private essences
but from the influence that they
radiate on their surroundings.
—C. H. Waddington

I have often felt in front of living beings—
above all in front of human heads—the sense
of space atmosphere which immediately
surrounds these beings, penetrates
them, is already the being themselves.
—A. Giacometti

When I encounter the work of Giacometti, the world becomes so much more unbearable. I think it is because this artist, in order to discover that which remains for man after all false exteriors are pealed off, does away with things that obstruct his vision. (···)

Beauty arises from nowhere but from the heart's wound. (···) Giacometti's art seems to discover the secret wound of all beings and things that brings light to them. (···) It brings forth an emotion close to terror and a lure that is almost as great.

—Jean Genet

An object that is deeply sensitive to changes in nature is an instrument for seeing anew the existing landscape. The reason we restrain from ornament is because architecture is the background for everyday life.

The word *emptiness* has a set of connotations not intended here—that sick and hollow feeling of loss or loneliness, the pain of hunger, and so forth. What is meant by emptiness here is rather more like...silence, clarity and transparency. Emptiness may resound without sound, may be filled by its potential to be filled, and make open what is complete.

Emptiness means *interval in space, interval in time* and *moment/place/occasion* all at once. Emptiness is in the gaps between stepping stones, though we might walk smoothly, in the silence between the notes of the song, though we might sing legato, or in the moment a pendulum reaches the top of its arc and stops without stopping.

—Michael Benedikt

While all human beings possess *xing* (an inborn nature), their *xin* (heart-minds) lack a fixed intention. It (that is, the heart-mind) depends on (external) things to become active; it depends on pleasure to become functioning; it depends on practice to become fixed. The *qi* of happiness, anger, sadness, and grief is (called) none other than nature. When it (that is, the *qi*) appears on the outside, it is because (external) things have laid hold of it. Human nature derives from the Mandate; the Mandate descends from Heaven. The *dao* begins in *qing*; *qing* (natural disposition) is derived from *xing* (human nature).
—*The Xing Zi Ming Chu*

While there are no stirrings of pleasure, anger, sorrow, or joy, the mind may be said to be in the state of Equilibrium. When those feelings have been stirred, and they act in their due degree, there ensues what may be called the state of Harmony. This Equilibrium is the great root from which grow all the human actings in the world, and this Harmony is the universal path which they all should pursue.
—*The Doctrine of the Mean*

(⋯) One must say that it is a state in which all emotion forms a dynamic equilibrium. The greatness of Zisi子思 lies not in stating the Mean as a moral act, the harmony of morality, but in stating the primacy of emotional energy.
—Kim Yong Ok

The space of emptiness is like *sincerity*,
and is thus a self-organizing becoming
that creates according to its internal and
external conditions. Sincerity is that
whereby self-completion is effected.

"Once is not enough."

I used to say as a kid.

That seemed very plausible to me,

"Once upon a time."

But when you take pictures,

I learned,

none of that applies.

Then "once" is

"once and for all."

—Wim Wenders

I want my water *madang* to
be like Monet's pond.

Everything in a stretch of water is new
when morning comes. What vitality the
chameleon-river must have to respond
so immediately to the kaleidoscope of
newborn light! The life of the trembling
water alone renews all the flowers. The
slightest movement of a quiet stream
provokes an array of floral beauty.
"Moving water, flowers the water's
hearbeats…" writes the poet. One flower
more complicates the whole stream. The
straighter the reed the lovelier the ripples.
And a young water iris, piercing the green
tangle of the water lilies, prompts the
painter immediately to share with us its
astonishing triumph. There it stands, every
sword drawn, every leaf a finely honed
blade, dangling its sulphurous tongue
with stinging irony high above the water.
A philospher musing before one of Monet's
water pictures might if he dared, develop
a dialectics of the iris and the water lily,
the dialectics of the string leaf and the
leaf which calmly, soberly, weightily
reposes upon the surface. It is the very
dialectics, surely, of the aquatic plant.
—Gaston Bachelard

Italo Calvino's *Invisible Cities* is an endless stimulant of my architectural imagination. Among them, three particular episodes:

CITIES & MEMORY 3

In vain, great-hearted Kubilai, shall I attempt to describe Zaira, city of high bastions. I could tell you how many steps make up the streets rising like stairways, and the degree of the arcades' curves, and what kind of zinc scales cover the roofs; but I already know this would be the same as telling you nothing.

The city does not consist of this, but of relationships between the measurements of its space and the events of its past: the height of a lamppost and the distance from the ground of a hanged usurper's swaying feet; the line strung from the lamppost to the railing opposite and the festoons that decorate the course of the queen's nuptial procession; the height of that railing and the leap of the adulterer who climbed over it at dawn; the tilt of the guttering and a cat's progress along it as he slips into the same window; the firing range of a gunboat which has suddenly appeared beyond the cape and the bomb that destroys the guttering; the rips in the fish net and the three old men seated on the dock mending nets and telling each other for the hundredth time the story of the gunboat of the usurper, who some say was the queen's illegitimate son, abandoned in his swaddling clothes there on the dock.

As this wave from memories flows in, the city soaks up like a sponge and expands. A description of Zaira as it is today should contain all Zaira's past. The city, however, does not tell its past, but contains it like the lines of a hand, written in the corners of the streets, the gratings of the windows, the banisters of the steps, the antennae of the lightning rods, the poles of the flags, every segment marked in turn with scratches, indentations, scrolls.

CITIES & DESIRE 5

From there, after six days and seven nights, you arrive at Zobeide, the white city, well exposed to the moon, with streets wound about themselves as in a skein. They tell this tale of its foundation: men of various nations had an identical dream. They saw a woman running at night through an unknown city; she was seen from behind, with long hair, and she was naked. They dreamed of pursuing her. As they twisted and turned, each of them lost her. After the dream they set out in search of that city; they never found it, but they found one another; they decided to build a city like the one in the dream.

In laying out the streets, each followed the course of his pursuit; at the spot where they had lost the fugitive's trail, they arranged spaces and walls differently from the dream, so she would be unable to escape again.

This is the city of Zobeide, where they settled, waiting for that scene to be repeated one night. None of them, asleep or awake, ever saw the woman again. The city's streets were streets where they went to work every day, with no link any more to the dreamed chase. Which, for that matter, had long been forgotten.

New men arrived from other lands, having had a dream like theirs, and in the city of Zobeide, they recognized something of the streets of dream, and they changed the position of arcades and stairways to resemble more closely the path of the pursued woman and so, at the spot where she had vanished, there would remain no avenue of escape.

The first to arrive could not understand what drew these people to Zobeide, this ugly city, this trap.

CITIES & THE SKY 3

Those who arrive at Thekla can see little of the city, beyond the plank fences, the sackcloth screens, the scaffolding, the metal armatures, the wooden catwalks hanging from the ropes or supported by saw-horses, the ladders, the trestles. If you ask, "why is Thekla's construction taking such a long time?" the inhabitants continue hoisting sacks, lowering leaded strings, moving long brushes up and down, as they answer, "So that its destruction cannot begin." And if asked whether they fear that, once the scaffolding is removed, the city may begin to crumble and fall to pieces, they add hastily, in a whisper, "Not only the city."

If dissatisfied with the answer, someone puts his eye to a crack in a fence, he sees cranes pulling up other cranes, scaffolding that embraces other scaffolding, beams that prop up other beams. 'What meaning does your construction have?' he asks. "What is the aim of a city under construction unless it is a city? Where is the plan you are following, the blueprint?"

"We will show it to you as soon as the working day is over; we cannot interrupt our work now," they answer.

Work stops at sunset. Darkness falls over the building site. The sky is filled with stars. "There is the blueprint," they say.

In Park Kyong-Ni's *Land*, where Yong
witnesses Wolseon's death, I dare say
that is the scene I most cherish.

The three people, overwhelmed by the
stern force overflowing from the whole
body, stood frozen at the spot. The door
opened and then shut. Yong, entering the
room, looked down at Wolseon. Wolseon
looked up at him as if blinded by light.
"I knew you would come."
Yong sits down next to Wolseon.
"I came after finishing work
on the hillsides."
Yong said as if plainly whispering.
"Yes, I knew you would."
"Dear."
His face buried close to her face. And
then he shivers. Like an aspen tree
that shivers from head to toe. After

a while, the quivering stopped.

"Dear."

"Yes."

"Stay still,"

Clearing the blanket, he folded her into his arms and lifted her on to his knees. A thin silver hairpin dropped from her hair to the floor.

"I'm cold, right?"

"No."

"We have lived long enough."

"Yes."

They look down and look up. Only the eyes are alive. Wolseon's body, light like a bird's feather, doesn't have the strength to hold on to Yong's sleeve.

"No regrets?"

"Yes, none at all."

"Then its okay. I also don't have any regrets."

Yong swept her hair. Her face had become so small. He swept her chin and laid her down quietly. With Yong back, Wolseon sustained herself for two nights. Wolseon passed away in the early morning a day after New Year's day.

Time is an unstoppable part of human destiny. With the flow of time, nature heals man-made wounds. Hence, the land of *grand memories* is a site of immense possibilities. We call this site Pyeonghwa-Nuri (Be Blessed with Peace). It is a humble preparation, a reconstructed landspace for solemn contemplation.

The traditional concept of space in Korea is a fusion of the natural philosophy of early Confucianism, Taoism, and the Zen philosophy of Buddhism. It is a philosophy of the co-existence of man and nature; one that perceives the universe, the earth, and man as a large singular organism. It perceived land as a vital and dynamic presence and considered man, together with the heavens and land, to be a constituent element of nature.

It is the spirit of the literati (*seonbi*) that created the Joseon space of self-disciplne. It systematized the cultural fusion of man the subject and nature the object into Confucian metaphysics and everyday practice. The spirit of the literati is a Taoist spirit and a spirit that practices loyalty. A literati values civility and honor as his own lifeblood. He would throw away his own life in order to protect justice.

The strength of this spirit kept our old and beautiful communities together and laid the foundation for our great spiritual heritage.

Kiohun, a secluded study hall in the rear garden of Changdeok-gung Palace, is literally a house where the literati trains the soul through persistent self-respect. Entering Geumma-mun Gate, located in front of Aeryeon-jeong Pavilion and next to Bullo-mun Gate, you see Kiohun and Uiduhab, two simple and elegant houses with half-hipped roofs. We know them to be the reading halls for the Crown Prince Hyomyeong. Unlike the exuberant pavilions within Changdeok-gung Palace, they are houses that are small but solid, humble but dignified and undiminished. The name Kiohun derives from the poem *The Gui Qu Lai Ci* by Tao Yuanming.

Leaning against the southern window, I look out with a strong heart. Though my knees barely fit into the small room, I know of its comfort.

Amidst nature's breadth and beauty, its footprint was made as small and as humble as possible. It is hence a house that honors nature, where the virtues of poverty and commonality are clearly manifest. It embodies the *seonbi*'s will to a fundamental world in which the heavens, earth, and man are one.

Madang

Beyond Aesthetics, Toward Ethics

Min Hyun Sik

My architecture begins with the idea of the "the *madang*[1] as a room." The *madang* is a key element in Korea's traditional architecture. It is a space that shows itself in "emptiness." In comparison to the "generic architectural space," it is relatively transparent and immaterial, and tends to be light and valueless.[2] It is similar to the condition of modern art, where the value of representational art has become null. There is a postmodern irony in that this aesthetic of disappearance is its very characteristic.

Here, there are questions concerning the nihilistic scent immersed in "emptiness." Nonetheless, the *madang*—the making of emptiness—provides an alternative beyond representational architecture. It constitutes a search for a dimension of architecture that goes beyond its objecthood.

I am an architect not a theorist. Hence, in the process of this search there are bound to be illogical jumps. I regard design as way of theorizing and in this sense I have always tried to define my work theoretically. However, there is an aspect of the work itself that cannot be approached with logic alone. Despite of the fact that my work moves within the context of Western modern architecture, it is simultaneously rooted in a totally opposite tradition—in the philosophy and methods of traditional Korean architecture. I believe, however, that contradiction and conflict can ignite creativity.

With this recognition, things that have caught my attention are collected from the vantage point of emptiness, from the universal history of architecture and the achievements of artists. Working to root "the making of emptiness" as a sound theory of architectural practice, different ideas are added and reorganized in creative ways.

The Function of Emptiness — Indeterminate Space

The empty *madang* is an indeterminate space.3 From a functionalist point-of-view, it has no predetermined function. In other words, the functionalist norm of "form follws function" does not apply. The *madang* is not a space where the intended function is realized.[4]

Indeterminate space is like a puzzle. It is a space waiting for something to happen, a space for solitude and congregation. Indeterminate space can be temporarily appropriated for needs that correspond to various purposes, densities, and changes in use.[5] The *madang* is not a design of form or system appropriate to function. It is a design of possibilities. The *madang* is designed with a sense of time.

As an infrastructure of daily life deeply imbedded in the properties and intimacies of the site—the fundamental character of site—it solidifies the characteristics of place and time, absorbs multiplicity, takes pleasure in pluralism, stirs the imagination, and finally, helps one enjoy indeterminacy and uncertainty.[6]

We want to see the truthfulness of space arise from uncertainty and unpredictability. We want its future users to ignite their potential and imagination and to use the resources and possibilities they already possess.

I believe in "not doing too much," in "almost doing nothing." If you do too much, you rob future users of their potential and imagination. The role of the architect must be limited to sowing seeds, creating agents, and generating programs that provide partial forecasts of their effects. This is the spatial economics and aesthetic condition of our present age. The essence of the *madang* lies in the structure of the platform. Like the *madang* itself, the mat is not a product designed in accordance with a specific function. It is temporary material that is augmented in variety and flexibility; that corresponds to changing situations of the space or place; that is determined by the user's occupancy. Hence, the platform must itself be an embodiment of adaptability and flexibility. Like the main circuit mother board whose fabric of microchips are hidden behind the surface the *madang* has the order of an electronic network. It has neither a fixed form nor a beginning and an end. It's essence lies in the constantly changing dynamic.[7] It is akin to contemporary sports that use flowing liquid as its medium. Hang-gliding, bungee-jumping, surfing and rafting are based on fluid-like flowing media, and share common features. These sports tend to be highly varied, changing, unpredictable, requiring sharp sensibilities, quick judgment and calculated risks.

The Aesthetic of Emptiness—Space of Specific Indeterminacy[8]

The *madang* partakes in a phenomenological aesthetics. The phenomenological attitude toward space and objects is based on the following logic.

> An insistence on the otherness of things, and the suggestion that what we know about them is not their own private essence—the Ding an Sich—but the influence they radiate on their surroundings...It seems quite plausible to me that it is like this because of the very fact that it is capable of existing—the fact that it does exist, that it is not crushed, scrubbed out, it seems to me that it is is necessary that there is a force which maintains it...[T]his force is...not simply an internal energy: it does not merely sustain a Presence, but is outgoing and has an impact on its surroundings.[9]

This attitude has the dual danger of perceiving the world, on the one hand, as a binary opposition between phenomena and essence, and on the other, as a phenomena or an unconsciousness that controls this phenomena. In overcoming these limitations, Alberto Giacometti's artistic intuition provides the key to the dialectic unification of these issues:

> I have often felt in front of living beings—above all in front of human heads—the sense of space atmosphere which immediately surrounds these beings, penetrates them, is already the being themselves.[10]

Perhaps it is because everything in the world has a decisive moment, we all experience those unexpected but precious moments when the ordinary world approaches us with a new freshness. The moment after the rain when sunlight shimmers on the asphalt road; when the twilight strikes the bell tower above the darkening trees that line the street; the moment you understand that "the apple is something that is really round!": these are moments that many poets have lyricised[11] and impressionists in particular have painted.[12] It is because photography was able to capture these unrepeatable moments that it was able to become an art.[13]

In these moments, it is not that our perceptions are overcome with sentimentalism. They are, on the contrary, matter-of-fact, neutral, and without desire. They overflow with inexplicable joy, as the phenomena and reality that are expressed coalesce with the evident rightness of things as they are. It first begins with a single sense but quickly spreads to all the other senses; finally, it trembles in every pore of the body. These experiences, these special moments are breathtaking. From these moments we can build the highest and most essential sense of an independent and meaningful reality. Michael Benedikt has called this "the direct aesthetic experience of reality."[14] Architecture and architectural space is not merely an object of visual pleasure but experienced through the five senses. The experience, at every moment, of a new feeling, that is the direct aesthetic experience of reality. Benedikt, who argues for the direct aesthetic experience of reality, describes the aesthetics of "emptiness" in the following manner.

> The word "emptiness" has a set of connotations not intended here—that sick and hollow feeling of loss or loneliness,[15] the pain of hunger, and so forth. What is meant by emptiness here is rather more like...silence, clarity and transparency. Emptiness may resound without sound, may be filled by its potential to be filled, and make open what is complete.
>
> Emptiness means "interval in space," "interval in time" and "moment/place/occasion" all at once. Emptiness is in the gaps between stepping stones, though we might walk smoothly, in the silence between the notes of the song, though we might sing legato, or in the moment a pendulum reaches the top of its arc and stops without stopping.[16]

Emptiness appears in the black ink painting of the Joseon Period and the paintings of Giorgio Morandi. It would be more accurate to say that these paintings design empty space than to say that they depict figures. More than the painted part it is the empty space left unpainted that is of consequence. Look at the ink brush techniques of the literati painting. It is closer to calligraphy than to painting in that it rejects representation. For the artist, calligraphy is a poetic expression of a particular relation. It is a kind of self-discipline and ritual in which the body and the painting surface meet at an elevated moment.

This is also readily found in the work of land artists. In his *La Mormaire*, Richard Serra created a connection between ten steel plates, and again, a connection between the land and the ten plates. It was an installation that enacted new possibilities on a "particular land or site."

Mies van der Rohe's crystal towers, by "almost doing nothing," sustain an aesthetic that leaves the object to be. His intended goal of "doing almost nothing with good things" constitutes an economy of aesthetics. Mies' work does not exist for itself. The changing moments of the seasons, the day and night of the city surround his work. When they are beautifully reflected and transfused, the reality of the work is revealed. Constantly changing under the play of light and air, from complete opacity to complete transparency, the transient conditions and the observer's mind lead us to anticipate a particular aesthetic experience.

Louis Kahn also discusses the way we are moved everyday by architecture's encounter with nature:

> We knew that the museum (building) would always be full of surprises. The blues would be one thing one day; the blues would be another thing another day, depending on the character of the light. Nothing static, nothing static as an electric bulb, which can only give you one iota of the character of light. So the museum (building) has as many moods as there are moments in time, and never as long as the museum remains as a building will there be a single day like the other. (⋯) A great American poet once asked the architect, "What slice of the sun does your building have? What light enters your room?"—As if to say the sun never knew how great it is until it struck the side of a building.[17]

From this point of view, the primary purpose of the *madang* is to create a happy relation with its immediate environment. Therefore, all of its particular conditions—the topography and layout of the land, the path of the sun, the flow of air, the surrounding landscape—become the conditions for the design of the *madang*.[18] A particular *madang*, from a functional point of view, may be no different from any other *madang* in that it is a neutral and indeterminate space. However, through the architect's observation, choice, and new interpretation, it gains a unique identity by forming a special relation with the particular environment. This is a specific indeterminate space.

The design of the *madang* is the act of editing the land; holding on to conditions inherent to the land and piecing all of them together to form a sensitive connection. Ultimately, it is not a spatial figure that is created by the *madang* but a relative connection to the other side of the land. Hence, the boundaries are taken apart in a flexible manner.

Likewise, the circulation of the *madang* need not be hierarchical or systematic. The actual movement deviates slightly from the anticipated flow, and at every moment, reveals a special unexpected landscape. Moving along this path, through the interior and exterior spaces whose boundaries have disintegrated, a captivating field of contradiction and tension is created. The whole has disappeared. With no defined beginning or end, we confront at every moment a sequence of landscapes. It may not be special. It may rather be an ordinary landscape set before fresh eyes; a low frame that reveals an opulent and floating city; a picturesque landscape of special trees, their barks aglow, lined along the neighbor's wall; a narrow alley-way lined with a textured wall. Look up and see afresh the fragmented sky of the city. Like a series of still photographs presented like a video, the conjunction of this landscape, carefully edited along the path of our movement, is a powerful force that awakens our everyday.

In the *madang*, there is a constant discord between space and everyday life, and hence a dynamic relation between the two. Such is the fundamental nature of life. Yet life exists not inside space but is ingrained in it, as if etched within. Together with the space it continues to move independently. When the life that momentarily occupied the space comes to an end, a sense of crisis emerges; that at any moment the space will together fall apart. However, at every turn, we confront a new aura. We thus understand that the space possesses its own unique and persistent quality.

This is possible because in the *madang* it is not the space itself that is intentionally designed but the connections and conditions. Hence, the categories of space and life are meaningless in this place. One could say that life was momentarily accommodated. But it could also be said that, with the cooperation of life, a particular atmosphere was created by the space. We do not merely enter the space by walking along the floor. One enters the space; but until space and life are stabilized as one entity, every moment generates discord. In the sense that the meaning of the *madang* is never directly present, that it is ever delayed and ever changing—an endless interchange of presence and absence—it is akin to Derrida's *différence*. The *madang* constitutes a cohabitation of contradiction, the discordance of spatial difference and temporal delay. It is a source of creation that simultaneously generates contradictions and embraces the confrontational subject and object.

The emotional landscape of the *madang* is a kind of ritual for that elevated moment when space and life meet. It is hence a space suffused with the possibilities of performances represented as appearance.

The Ethics of Emptiness

The *madang*, where emptiness has been made, does not have a fixed figure that performs a prefigured function. It is a space of un-presented possibilities. It has the consistent character of timely change. Its incessant transformation implies that it is a thing of Continuous Creation 生生不息," that never ceases to produce difference.

It is the space of Equilibrium中.[19] This "space of emptiness," as an un-presented condition, is like a self-creating Sincerity誠. Therefore, according to the conditions of the interior and exterior, it is a space of self-organizing becoming that self-creates.[20] It is akin to Anaximander's apeiron.[21] It is Deleuze's "body without organ (CsO)": that which incessantly pursues deterritorialization. It is a great reversal of 2,500 years of Platonic Western thought; via Bergson's rediscovery of Heraclitus, it constitutes the exuberant rebirth of the Greek philosopher of generation and change. "Here, emptiness does not mean that something is absent. It is a cognitive 'emptiness' that belies purity un-clouded by a pinch of wickedness. Because it is empty, we can respond to all sense data without prejudice."[22]

The Joseon literati (seonbi) paid special attention to the spatial character of Continuous Creation. The spatial beauty of the schools, houses, and pavilions they created lies not in the space itself. The beauty of this space, communicating with a grand, ever-changing nature, creates difference. It is a beauty whose essence lies in the constant change of creative creation. This is so because "that which is" is "that which ceaselessly changes."[23]

If we remind ourselves that thinking difference and change is a process of constant self-negation, this space provides a path beyond aesthetics and toward ethics. It is a space like the leaves and waves that dance in light and air. It was a space of self-reflection, what the seonbi called the space of self-discipline.[24]

At such a moment, we must study the Korean peninsular's particular topography, the way Korea's traditional philosophy of nature viewed the space that it created, and finally, based on this philosophy, the attitude toward how such land should be occupied.

Look at the old maps of Korea that illuminate the structure of the peninsular's landscape. Traditional Korean geography (construed by its maps and geographical reports), during the later Joseon Period, characteristically viewed the land as an organic construction of san'gyeong (the continuous flow of mountain ridgelines) and su'gyeong (the flow of water created by the watershed ridgelines). Though the map is drawn in two dimensions, we see it as a great land-space, a three-dimensional landscape constructed by the flow of mountains and rivers. In this unique landscape, we see the life of the Korean people, choose land for cultivation, open roads, build houses, and create villages and towns.

This old concept of space is a synthesis of primitive Confucianism, Taoist view of nature, and Buddhist Zen philosophy. It is a philosophy that perceives heaven, earth and man as one, a philosophy of the co-existence of man and nature.[25] This is the philosophy of the Balance of Man and Thing人物均.[26] Koreans viewed the land as living and dynamic, a being of Continuous Creation. Together with the earth and the heavens, man was considered to be constituent of nature. Land was understood as the infrastructure for the artificial constructions of buildings and cities, as a space full of emerging properties, of possibilities waiting to be territorialized and occupied by man.

From this point of view, the boundary between nature and man, between natural space and artificial space falls apart. The modern project of creating a characteristic environment through an architectural collective shifts toward the task of deriving the architectural conditions from the conditions of the environment and the land. Instead of viewing architecture as an object, the latter views it as one constituent element of the environment. Hence, attention is paid less to architecture itself and more to the relation between building and building, between architecture and the environment.

In creating a house, instead of calling for the will of the architect, the environment is carefully observed, and from this observation, a set of conditions are derived and then used. Instead of approaching architecture as an object, the new architectural landscape is managed by adding a house to the existing landscape. There is a period of refinement as the new house and the environment is in constant interaction. The expectation is that one day the new house will have been transformed into an element of the environment.[27] Instead of creating the environment, an attitude true to an ethical consciousness toward the existing environment emerges. This kind of thinking and attitude provides the path to a practice that moves beyond an architecture of representation; that is, an architecture that moves beyond the horizon of objectification.

Furthermore, as this space of self-discipline is managed, the space occupied within a broad, beautiful nature is minimized and simplified. Every effort is given to the respect of nature, to the manifestation of commonality and the virtue of poverty. It is the path of the ethics of nature and man—the path of the spirit of the Strong Heart寄傲.[28]

This path, through an endless repetition of negation and the process of reflexive interpretation, is made to slowly approach the real thing. This is the very process of structuring emptiness. Through the transformations of visual perception and the mechanisms of understanding, objectivity is repeatedly eliminated. With the simultaneous process of evocation, one may reach the goal of *sunyata*. It is the wish to reach Great Emptiness太虛.

Beyond an Architecture of Representation

Based on reason and freedom, the modern project dreamt of "a better world." In contradiction to this utopian hope, the last century became a betrayal of the promise of reason. Bathed in violence and war, it has ended up a spectacular counter to freedom and independence.[29] As life reveals itself as a great accumulation of spectacle, things that were directly constituent of life retreat into representation. "[Capitalism] has resolved personal worth into exchange value... All that is solid melts into the air, all that is holy is profaned."[30] Capitalism has degraded being into having, into mere appearance. Architecture and the city, as if solid, stands at its forefront.

In the society of the spectacle, being is always and everywhere mediated by images designed to promote passive consumption, and hence to take away direct experience, feelings, and connections from our lives. We have been forced to adjust to lives dictated by our architecture[31] and to become a passive audience that merely looks on. This is a lie that has imprisoned time into space. The society of the spectacle cannot be regarded merely as the product of the misuse of the visual world or the result of the technology of the mass distribution of images. On the contrary, it is a practicality, an objectified world-view, a world-view translated through matter.

Moreover, the present seeks once again to distinguish itself from the past. If the society of the spectacle was constituted by a landscape of original objects, they are now being replaced by simulacra.[32] Lee Jeong Woo has claimed that "recently, the world has passed through a temporal hinge in which one era has ended and a new one has begun... It is a new 'era of the simulacra.' The computer and the video are the primary machines that have made this possible. As these machines have dominated everyday life, the simulacra has overwhelmed the world... the traditional simulacra of language and pictures have taken a back seat as the images and events created through simulation have filled the cultural forefront. The rise of simulation has energized modern culture (particularly in terms of its aesthetics), but it has simultaneously driven the age of modernity into a dream state... The relation between life and the dream has been reversed."[33] But certainly for the present age, which prefers the sign to the thing signified, the copy to the original, fancy to reality, appearance to essence, this change, inasmuch as it does away with illusion, is an absolute annihilation, or at least a reckless profanation; for in these days illusion is sacred and truth is profane. The sacred is enhanced in as much as truth decreases and illusion increases, and as a result, the highest degree of illusion results in the highest degree of sacredness.[34]

However, from the beginning of the modern project, the seed to its counter-movement—the escape to its beyond—was born within the project. The solid castle of metaphysics built up by Plato and Descartes was destroyed by the nineteenth-century masters of suspicion—Henri Bergson, Friedrich Nietzsche, Karl Marx, and Sigmund Freud. Writers such as James Joyce, Virginia Woolf, and T. S. Eliot were already aware of the moving impressions, schizophrenic desires, primary forces, unconscious stimuli, bodily feelings, and sensuous emotions that departed from the judgment and reason of the subject. Paradoxically, leaning on these crumpled, unrecognized boundaries—non-being, indeterminacy, virtuality, the non-real, meaninglessness, generation, simulacra—are fleeing to places conceptualization cannot reach. It attempted to overthrow the millennia old formula of the "supremacy of reason over aesthesis (sensuous perception)," a project that is now becoming reality. Feeling has a certain fundamental capacity that emerges before reason, that emerges from its basis and makes the latter possible. Therefore, sense is an existential event in which the sensory organs descend directly to the body. It is a materialist event generated like a "vibration"[35] that is felt through every cell of the body, felt on the osmotic surface where the life body meets its environment.

With this view of the twenty-first century, let us re-examine the ground of architecture. Let us go beyond the twentieth-century spectacle of representational architecture, to a memory sympathetic to nature that existed before the emergence of all value. As the emptiness of an un-presented world of feelings returns to a *built* architecture, I strive for a kind of architecture that goes beyond the horizon of objectification; a move toward an architecture of life committed to the working living system.[36] I wish it to be the responsibility and ethics of the architecture of our era.

Notes

1   "Making Emptiness" is a term that is still very awkward, a term that feels a bit disorganized. When I first began writing this essay, it was titled "Structuring Emptiness." It was the title for the Min Hyunsik + Seung H-Sang Architecture Exhibition hosted by the University of Pennslyvania in 2002 and also the title of the book written together with Seung H-Sang and Khang Hyuk. We have here two words—emptiness and building—that are paradoxically juxtaposed. The *madang* that I am talking about is not concerned with the figure of architecture but with its ground, and hence I feel that "making" is more appropriate than "structuring."

By reversing the usual architectural "figure/ground" into a "ground/figure," it approaches architecture as an organism. An organism has the wonderful characteristic of autopoiesis (self-production). I wish to point to the fact that it emerges through its own force and, through its own activity, gradually detaching itself from the environment (Humberto Maturana and Francisco Varela, *El árbol del conocimiento*). How arbitrary it is that, within a complex network of connections, we draw a boundary around a pattern, isolate the pattern, and then call it an "object."

In Ancient Greek, *architectonicé* (architecture) meant *architectonicé techné*. *Architectonicé techné* is the *techné* of the *architectón* which is a combination of *arché* (origin, principle, the primary) and *tectón* (craftsman). Among Greeks, architecture was considered not merely a skill of craftsmen but an art practiced by those who possess a principal knowledge and mastery of all technologies, and who therefore plan projects and lead other craftsmen. In this context the term *techné* meant not only technology in a narrow sense but also *poesis* (making) in general. Plato defined it in the following way: "By the original meaning *poiesis* means simply creation, and creation as you know, can take very various forms. Any action which is the cause of a thing emerging from non-existence into existence might be called *poiesis*, and all the processes in all the crafts are kinds of *poiesis* , and all those who are engage in them *creators*." In the metaphor of architecture Plato discovered a figure that under the aegis of "making" is able to withstand "becoming." (Kojin Karatani, *Architecture as Metaphor*, Cambridge: MIT Press, 1995, pp.5-6.)

The Japanese, Chinese, Korean translation of "architecture" into "*geonchuk*建築" (to erect and to pile) leans toward one aspect of architecture and thus leaves much to be desired. It inherently has the danger of treating architecture as an object of representation and thus figuring it as spectacle. Koreans have traditionally used the term *yeongjo*營造 and *jid'da*짓다 or *jiem*지음, terms which seem closest to the essence of architecture. The architectural practice that we have long sustained is defined in the Korean dictionary below.

[jid'da짓다] (1) to make a meal, clothes, or a house.

(2) to make medicine by mixing various ingredients

(3) to write a poem, novel, letter, or lyrics of a song

(4) to gather and form a line or formation

(5) to farm a dry or wet land

(6) to form and create a falsity

(7) to show an expression or attitude in a face or body

(8) to make a knot by stringing together or tying up

(9) to commit a crime

(10) to make a decision or finalize a continuing task or speech

(11) to name

(12) to form a relation or coupling

[synonyms] to farm / to speak / to grow / to write / to edit / to do / to erect / to formulate

2   For example, Le Corbusier's definition that "Architecture is the masterful, correct and magnificent play of masses, brought together in light" can be understood within the tradition of Western thought in which light serves as a metaphor of truth.

3   Indeterminate space is at times called an indefinite space or an uncommitted or free space (C. Price). Mies Van Der Rohe's universal space is also such a space.

4   The notion of realization here expresses Plato's ontology. The concepts that appear later—such as "embodiment化身" "incarnation化體" "presence顯現" "concretization具體化" "reflection體化" "materialization體現"—all contain a similar nuance. Though the presence of Plato's "Idea" may be characterized as a certain immateriality, that is loss of materiality (corporality), the notion of "the incarnation of the word" in Christianity and Islam constitutes the essence of traditional Western thought.

In Platonic Realism the eternal object constitutes a kind of entelecheia現實態 and actual entity that exists independently. However, in the modern philosophy of science (represented by the thought of A. N. Whitehead) the eternal object is not an ontological entity but has primary meaning as pure potentials可能態. Pure potentials constitute indeterminateness. Therefore the actual entity emerges by choosing (or deciding on) one of these indeterminate possibilities. This choice is itself a becoming and an ingression into the eternal object.

5 Our goal is to pursue architectural space as a room, a room where man can spread its imagination. Its character is defined by context, place, and material, not by the combination of anticipated function. It will be able to house unknown uses of the future.

6 "While there are no stirrings of pleasure, anger, sorrow, or joy, the mind may be said to be in the state of Equilibrium中. when those feelings have been stirred, and they act in their due degree, there ensues what may be called the state of Harmony和
(喜怒哀樂之未發 謂之中 發而皆中節 謂之和)."
(Confucius, Translated by James Legge, *500 BC The Doctrine of the Mean Confucius*, 1893.)

7 The universe is an organic universe, not a field where dead material moves about. Therefore, there cannot but be senses in all universal conditions. This is a concept that encompasses modern physics, especially ideas such as interaction in the electro-magnetic field.

8 It may seem paradoxical to say that something is both particular and indeterminate. We usually consider a space to be general, multi-purpose, and of a generic design if the use is not the main determinate to desiging the space. This is where the danger lies. When particularity is excluded, it can only result in a characterless building or a black box.

"This specificity of space comes from the place. A heightened awareness of a situation needs to be created. Attraction, and charge can come about by generating a new view of an adjacent large or small space, to a landscape or a piece of town, perhaps as a momentary glimpse. Giving measure to an existing topography, making new connections within a given place, offering a safe degree of danger or excitement, revealing lost information, are other ways of giving attention and specificity to the space." (Florian Beigel, "Brikettfabrik Witznitz: Specific Indeterminacy—Designing for Uncertainty," *ARQ* 2. Dec. 1996.)

9 C. H. Waddington, *Behind Appearance: A Study of the Relations Between Painting and the Natural Sciences in this Century*, Edinburgh: Edinburgh University Press, 1970, pp.232-234.

10 C. H. Waddington, *Behind Appearance: A Study of the Relations Between Painting and the Natural Sciences in this Century*, Edinburgh: Edinburgh University Press, 1970.

11 "Until I spoke your name, you had been no more than a mere gesture. When I spoke your name, you came to me and became a flower. Now speak my name, one fitting this color and odor of mine, as I spoke your name, so that I may go to you and become your flower. We all wish to become something, You to me and I to you wish to become an unforgettable gaze."(Kim Chun-Su, "Flower.")

12 Gaston Bachelard, *The Right to Dream*, Dallas: The Dallas Institute of Humanities and Culture, 1989, pp. 4-5.

13 "Still, each and every moment of picture-taking, Wherever in the world it takes place, is a single event, its uniqueness guaranteed by the incessant progress of time... 'Once is not enough,' I used to say as a kid. That seemed very plausible to me, 'Once upon a time.' But when you take pictures, I learned, none of that applies. Then once is once and for all." (Wim Wenders, *Once: Picture and Stories*, New York: DAP, 2001. p.267.)

14 "Direct aesthetic experience of reality." Michael Benedikt, *For an Architecture of Reality*, Lumen Books, 1987.

The direct aesthetic experience of reality is not simply limited to the physical elements of the environment but involves its totality through the involvement of our character.

"I was on the way to school. I looked up and saw the mysterious harmony of the bright young leaves and the sunlight—. An outing together: my father in a black serge topcoat and my pretty mother, always walking slightly in the distance, in a jade woolen top —. Last day of December, the row of dumplings on the tray—. The day my big brothers, Hyeok and Uk first had their suits tailor-made; how handsome they were—. My mother's things which I and my mother both loved: the white sable fur scarf and thick golden ring that she always wore—. The purple Paulownia flowers dropping in the courtyard on a sunny day—." (Park Wan-Suh, *The Naked Tree*, Youlhwadang Publishers, 2012, p.121.)

15 Michael Benedikt does not further explicate his notion of 'nothingness', but it is clear that Nietzsche's nihilism is imbedded in his thinking.

16 Michael Benedikt, *For an Architecture of Reality*, Lumen Books, 1987.
Michael Benedikt, *Deconstructing the Kimbell: An Essay on Meaning and Architecture*, Sites Books, 1992.

17 Nell E. Johnson, *Light Is the Theme: Louis I*

Kahn and the Kimbell Art Museum, Kimbell Art Museum, 1975.

18　"We are both storytellers. Lying on our backs, we look up at the night sky. This is where stories began, under the aegis of that multitude of stars which at night filch certitudes and sometimes return them as faith. Those who first invented and then named the constellations were storytellers. Tracing an imaginary line between a cluster of stars gave them an image and an identity. The stars threaded on a narrative. Imagining the constellations did not of course change the stars, nor did it change the black emptiness that surrounds them. What it changed was the way people read the night sky." (John Berger, *And Our Faces, My Heart, Brief as Photos*, Vintage, 1992.)

19　See note 6.

20　"Without sincerity there would be nothing. Sincerity is that whereby self-completion is effected (不誠無物 誠者自成也)." (『中庸』 25; Confucius, Translated by James Legge, *500 BC The Doctrine of the Mean Confucius*, 1893.)

　　"In his *Critique of Judgement* Kant discussed the nature of living organisms. He argued that organisms, in contrast with machines, are self-reproducing, self-organizing wholes. In a machine, according to Kant, the parts only exist for each other, in the sense of supporting each other within a functional whole. In an organism the parts also exist by means of each other, in the sense of producing one another. We must think of each part as an organ, wrote Kant, "that produces the other parts (so that each reciprocally produces the other).... Because of this, 'The organism' will be both an organized and self-organizing being." (Fritjof Capra, *The Web of Life*, Anchor Books, p. 21.)

21　"Apeiron is a kind of X. It is an undefined, non-consistent, non-confining something, still undefined as water, fire, air, earth. Yet it is a something that can be defined, or differentiated, to use a latter day term, as these four things. In this aspect, apeiron is without peras; that is, it is without boundary, limit, division, confinement, and definition. Apeiron is that which has not received these things. That the undetermined is determined and thus becomes a certain thing...." (Lee Jeong Woo, *History of World Philosophy* 1, Gil Publishing, 2011, pp.69-70.)

22　Kim Yong Ok, *Korean Commentary on the Doctrine of the Mean*, Tongnamu Publishing, 2011, p.159.

23　"Hence to entire sincerity there belongs ceaselessness (故至誠無息)." (Confucius, Translated by James Legge, *500 BC The Doctrine of the Mean Confucius*, 1893.)

24　"There is nothing more visible than what is secret, and nothing more manifest than what is minute. Therefore the superior man is watchful over himself, when he is alone. (是故君子戒愼乎其所不賭 恐懼乎其所不聞 莫見乎隱 莫顯乎微 故君子愼其獨也)." (Confucius, Translated by James Legge, *500 BC The Doctrine of the Mean Confucius*, 1893.)

25　"The saint is a synthesis of the heavens and earth, and obviously the common man is also the synthesis of the heavens and earth. It is not just man but all things that are the synthesis of the heavens and earth." (Kim Yong Ok, *Korean Commentary on the Doctrine of the Mean*, Tongnamu Publishing, 2011, p.579.)

　　This kind of thinking is not confined to the East. Spinoza had similar thoughts: "Man in part of Nature and must follow its laws, and this alone is true worship. There is only one kingdom in Spinoza's world, the kingdom of God, or Nature; and human beings belong to this kingdom in the same way that stones, trees, and cats do." (Matthew Stewart, *The Courtier and the Heretic: Lebniz, Spinoza, and the fate of God in the Modern World*, W. W. Norton & Company, 2007.)

26　Fritjof Capra argued that "the whole question of values is crucial to deep ecology; it is, in fact, it's central defining characteristics. Whereas the old paradigm is based on anthropocentric (human-centered) values, deep ecology is grounded in ecocentric (earth-centered) values. It is a worldview that acknowledges the inherent value of nonhuman life. All living beings are members of ecological communities bound together in a network of interdependencies. When this deep ecological perception becomes part of our daily awareness, a radically new system of ethics emerges." (Fritjof Capra, *The Web of Life*, Anchor Books, p. 11.)

　　"This had long before been asserted by the ecological thinkers of the Joseon period: the understanding of the eco-system as a grand field of life, a large field of harmony and coexistence (Maewoldang Kim Si Seub 梅月堂 金時習); the perspective of the Balance of Man and Thing, that man and thing are fundamentally equal with no hierarchy in value (Damheon Hong Dae Yong 湛軒 洪大容). This was a search for a new ethics in the relation between man and other living things. By acknowledging the individuality of the relation between man and man,

man and thing, and thing and thing, it moves beyond the differentiation of the other and develops an ideology of equality and an ethics that respects the life of each individual being." (Park Hee Byeong, *The Ecological Thought of Korea*, Dolbegae Publishing, 1999.)

27 "In becoming architects, we learn to see the world with intelligent sensuality. Intuitive propositions become the means by which we discover the qualities of location: architectural moves, in anticipation, indicate the frame we call it 'site'. In reciprocal process, the proposition and the location each becomes a measure of each other. The unique circumstances of a situation invoke the sensual intelligence with which a strategic insight is accurately developed to an eloquent existence." (Jeanne Sillett, *Macdonald and Salter: Building Projects, 1982-86 Mega III*, Architectural Association Publications, 1987.)

28 "Leaning against the southern window, I look out with a strong heart. Though my knees barely fit into the small room, I know of its comfort (倚南窗以寄傲 審容膝以易安)." (Tao Yuanming, *The Gui Qu Lai Ci*)

29 "The seventeenth Century was the age of mathematics, the eighteenth century the age of physics, and the nineteenth century the age of biology, the twentieth century is the age of terror." (Albert Camus, *Actuelles. Écrits politiques*, Gallimard, 1950; Paul Virilio, *L'Art à perte de vue*, Galilée, 2005.) Hannah Arendt defines the twentieth century as an age of violence.

30 "It has resolved personal worth into exchange value, (···) All that is solid melts into the air, all that is holy is profaned, an man is at last compelled to face with sober senses his real conditions of life and his relations with his kind." (Karl Marx and Friedrich Engels, *The Communist Manifesto*. Penguin Books, p.223.)

31 "We shape our buildings, thereafter they shape us." (Winston Churchill, *Time*, June 1960.)

32 "Primary things such as the heavens and earth, water and fire, animals and plants stood clearly before man with a sturdy reality." (Lee Jeong Woo, *The Battle of the Gods and the Titans*, Hangilsa, 2008, p.57.)

33 Lee Jeong Woo, *The Battle of the Gods and the Titans*, Hangilsa, 2008, pp.59-61.

34 Ludwig Feuerbach, *The Essence of Christianity*, Preface to second edition, 1843.

35 A vibration that repeats itself in almost (but not totally) the same manner; one that creates, at first glance, a seemingly arbitrary pattern, but which is actually complex and highly organized.

36 During this century the change from the mechanistic to the ecological paradigm has proceeded in different speeds in the various scientific fields. It in not a steady change. It involves scientific revolutions, backlashes, and pendulum swings. (Fritjof Capra, *The Web of Life*, Anchor Books, p.36.) This is very similar to the Asian Philosophy in "The Doctrine of the Mean."

List of Photographs

Photo Credits

Young-Soo Kim 122-123; Jong Oh Kim 10-11, 14-17, 23, 27, 36-37, 42-43, 47-52, 56-57, 66-67, 74-75, 78-81, 86-91, 95-101, 106-107, 110-113, 118-119, 126-129, 132-139; Daejeon Unversity 39; Bona Park 117; Park Young Chea 44-45; Min Hyun Sik 12-13, 32-33, 68-69, 108-109, 121, 130-131; Ahn Sekwon 84-85; Lee Seung Yun 21, 60, 76-77; Lim Jeung Eui 58-59; Chang Suk-Chul 142-143; Young Joon Chung 70-71; Choi Yun Hee 8-9; Choi Hee Jung 29, 35, 38, 61; Tak Chungseok 120.

Quotation Sources

16 Paul Bourget, *Le démon de midi*, Paris: Plon, 1914, p.375.

18 Mies van der Rohe, "Introductory Remarks to the Special Issue 'Werkbundausstellung: Die Wohnung'," Friz Neumeyer, trans. Mark Jarzombek, *The Artless Word: Mies van der Rohe on the Building Art*, Cambridge: MIT Press, 1994, p.258.

19 Song Giwon, "A Few Words about Ha Jong O," Ha Jong O, *From April to May*, Seoul: Changbi Publishers, 1984, pp.161-162.

26 (Top) Christian Norberg-Schulz, "A Talk with Mies van der Rohe," in Friz Neumeyer, trans. Mark Jarzombek, *The Artless Word: Mies van der Rohe on the Building Art*, Cambridge: MIT Press, 1994; first published in "Ein Gespräch mit Mies van der Rohe," in *Baukunst und Werkform*, no. 11, Nürnberger Presse, 1958.

26 (Bottom) Friz Neumeyer, trans. Mark Jarzombek, *The Artless Word: Mies van der Rohe on the Building Art*, Cambridge: MIT Press, 1994.

28 (Top) Pier Vittorio Aureli, *Brussels: A Manifesto Towards the Capital of Europe*, Rotterdam: NAi Publishers, 2007, p.7.

28 (Bottom) Rem Koolhaas, *S, M, L, XL*, New York: The Monacelli Press, 1995.

34 Park Hee Byeong, *Ecological Thought of Korea*, Seoul: Dolbegae Publishing, 1999.

40 David Harvey, *Paris, Capital of Modernity*, Routledge, 2003.

41 Chun Jin-Sung, *History Speaks of Memory*, Seoul: Humanist Books, 2005, p.39, p.42.

53 Umberto Eco, *The Name of the Rose*, New York: A Harvest Book-Harcourt, Inc. 1984, p.72.

54 René Burri, *Luis Barragán*, London: Phaidon, 2000, p.23.

63 Yevgeny Vinokurov, ed. and trans. Daniel Weissbort, *Post-War Russian Poetry*, New York: Penguin Books, 1974, p.103.

73 Nell E. Johnson, *Light Is the Theme: Louis I. Kahn and the Kimbell Art Museum*, Texas: Kimbell Art Museum, 1975.

82 C. H. Waddington, *Behind Appearance: A Study of the Relations Between Painting and the Natural Sciences in This Century*, Edinburgh: Edinburgh University Press, 1970.

83 Jean Genet, *L'Atelier d'Alberto Giacometti*, Paris: Gallimard, 2007. pp.14-15.

92 (Top) Michael Benedikt, *For an Architecture of Reality*, Santa Fe: Lumen Books, 1987, p.50.

92 (Bottom) Michael Benedikt, *Deconstructing the Kimbell: An Essay on Meaning and Architecture*, Sites Books, 1992, p.10.

93 (Left) Shirley Chan, "Human Nature and Moral Cultivation in the Guodian (郭店), Text of the *Xing Zi Ming Chu* (性自命出, *Nature Derives from Mandate*)," *Dao*, Volume 8, Issue 4, Springer Netherlands, pp.361-382.

93 (Right top) Confucius, trans. James Legg, *500 BC The Doctrine of the Mean Confucius*, 1893. Chapter 1-4.

93 (Right bottom) Kim Yong Ok, *Korean Commentary on the Doctrine of the Mean*, Seoul: Tongnamu Publishing, 2011, pp.246-247.

104 Wim Wenders, *Once: Pictures and Stories*, New York: DAP, 2001, p.267.

105 Gaston Bachelard, trans. J. A. Underwood, *The Right to Dream*, Dallas: The Dallas Institute of Humanities and Culture, 1989. pp.4-5.

114-116 Italo Calvino, trans. William Weaver, *Invisible Cities*, New York: Picador, 1979. pp.13, 39, 101.

124-125 Park Kyong-Ni, *Land*, Vol.4. Seoul: Jisik-sanup Publishing, 1979, p.388.

Min Hyun Sik

FKIA, Hon. FAIA

Min Hyun Sik was born in 1946, Korea. After receiving a BS from Seoul National University in 1970, he worked and studied under Kim Swoo Geun and Yoon Seung Joong. In 1989/90, he studied at the AA School of Architecture in London, UK. In 1992, he started his own practice H. Min Architect and Associates. In 1997, he was a founding member of School of Visual Arts, The Korea National University of Arts, where has taught as a professor until 2012. Since "Housing with Deep Space" exhibited in *Echoes of an Era*, he has been active in the public arena. Extending his architectural interests into urbanism, he participated in several urban planning and design projects such as the "Paju Landscape Script" for Paju Bookcity, "Gwangju, Asian Cultural Capital City," "Suwon, Historical and Cultural City," "Maemooldo Island, Love to Visit" etc. Through works, publications, teaching, and international exhibitions such as the Venice Biennale (2000/02), "Structuring Emptiness" at U-Penn (2003), S(e)oulscape (2008-9), his creative ideas have been at the center of important transitional moments in Korean Architecture and Urbanism.
www.minhyunsik.com

Pai Hyungmin

Professor, University of Seoul

Pai Hyungmin received his Ph.D at MIT and is a two-time Fulbright Scholar. He is author of *The Portfolio and the Diagram* (2002), *Sensuous Plan: The Architecture of Seung H-Sang* (2007), and *The Key Concepts of Korean Architecture* (2012). He has curated numerous major exhibitions among which the Korean Pavilion for the 2014 Venice Biennale won the Golden Lion.

Min Hyun Sik Architecture 1987–2012 © 2015 by Min Hyun Sik
Korean Edition © 2012 by Min Hyun Sik

Translation: Pai Hyung Min
Editor: Yi Soojung
Designers: Chung Byung Kyu, Bak Soyoung

Published by Youlhwadang Publishers.
Paju Bookcity, Gwanginsa-gil 25, Paju-si, Gyeonggi-do, Korea
Tel +82-31-955-7000 Fax +82-31-955-7010
www.youlhwadang.co.kr yhdp@youlhwadang.co.kr

ISBN 978-89-301-0467-8
Printed in Korea.

This book was published with the support of Arts Council Korea